The Adventures of Obi and Titi

Shango's Axe of Thunder

Written by O.T Begho

'Shango's Axe of Thunder'

Copyright © 2017 O.T Begho

Cover design and illustrations by O.T Begho

Published in Great Britain by
Evolution Media Lab Ltd

First Printing: 2017

ISBN: 978-0-9554966-5-3

www.obiandtiti.com

Note to readers

At the end of this book, you will find a list of words and their definitions. You can also find more amazing facts about Africa and some of the places described in this book on our website at www.obiandtiti.com.

Prologue

Who would have thought that a harmless game of hide and seek would have led to Obi and Titi setting off on a magical adventure across the Benin kingdom?

With the help of the mysterious masked rider, the children had narrowly escaped from Ile-Ife and had been able to save the Queen, Titi's aunt.

Obi had been reunited with his father, but their reunion was short-lived as Ezomo was still hot on their heels. Unfortunately, things were going from bad to worse as they had all been separated and Titi had been captured and was now in the hands of Ezomo.

Contents

Chapter 1

Mumu to the Rescue

Chapter 2

From Dusk Till Dawn

Chapter 3

Ezomo, the Past, Present and Future

Chapter 4

The Seven Okutas

Vocabulary

African Facts

Chapter 1

Mumu to the Rescue

Obi had miraculously survived his jump off the cliff. The water was freezing, but that was the least of his worries. He had heard Titi scream and as he looked up he could see Ezomo pushing someone over the edge of the cliff. He tried to swim back, but the current was too strong. The body that had just fallen into the water was heading toward him. He gave a deep sigh of relief as it passed. It wasn't Titi but then he remembered Idia.

Obi turned around and started swimming with the current. He could see Idia's head bobbing in and out of the water ahead. She had nearly reached the rocks. It took Obi a few minutes, but he was able to catch up with her just in time. He could see she was still breathing, but her head had a deep gash. He couldn't worry about that now, the water was getting choppy, and the rocks were only a few feet away.

Obi put both his arms around Idia's neck then used his legs to push himself and Idia sideways, just managing to avoid the rocks, whilst keeping her head above water. Obi was able to get a foothold, as the water in this part was about waist height, but the current was still very strong and was pushing them closer and closer to the waterfall.

"I'm coming, oh!" came a squeaky voice from behind him.

It was Mumu. He was paddling towards them on a large tree branch, which he had cleverly tied to a long vine. The vine had reached its full length, so it was up to Obi to walk back to reach him.

"Well done Mumu," Obi said, pushing Idia on top of the log, but as he tried to get on, it began to move again.

"Mumu, did you tie the other end?" Obi asked.

"Errr," Mumu said, as they both looked back and watched the end of the vine slipping into the water.

Before they knew it they were all hurtling, at full speed, toward the edge of the waterfall. Obi grabbed Idia tightly and took a deep breath. He knew if they were to survive the fall he would have to get her up to the surface as quickly as possible.

Obi hit the water hard. It felt like his chest had been stomped on by an elephant and he could feel the air being squeezed out of his lungs. It was taking every bit of energy in him to stop from blacking out. He shook his head to keep awake and started kicking frantically, swimming to the surface and pulling Idia up behind him.

"It's going to be okay," Obi said, after breaking the surface and swimming as hard as he could toward the bank.

"Help oh, I'm drowning!" shouted Mumu, splashing around hysterically behind him.

"Open your eyes," Obi shouted back, pointing to the log floating right next to Mumu. "You need to learn how to swim."

"Please oh, a swimming monkey, who has ever heard of such a ridiculous thing?"

Obi reached the bank and pulled Idia out.

She was still breathing, but barely. Her eyes and lips were turning white and Obi could see the cut on the side of her head was still bleeding.

"Obi," Idia said, drowsily. "You must run."

"Shhh," Obi replied, ignoring her.

He closed his eyes and laid them on the side of her head and concentrated. He could feel his hands becoming warm, but before he knew it he had blacked out.

A few minutes later he could hear voices and felt his face being slapped.

"Obi, Obi, I told you to run. You never listen."

Obi opened his eyes. He could see Idia staring down at him and Mumu standing behind her.

"Obi will never listen, oh. Words go in one ear and out the other, like diarrhoea,"

Mumu said walking off to find something to eat.

"We have to go and get Titi. Ezomo has her," Obi said, sitting up.

He began relaying the series of events that took place just after Idia had fallen off the cliff.

"We can't go back, Obi. We have to keep moving."

"No, we can't leave her," he said angrily.

"Obi listen, Ezomo won't harm her. Remember when he caught you in the palace, what did you say Mumu overheard him saying?"

"He told his men to do away with Mumu and I but take Titi alive."

"Exactly! Whatever his plan is, he needs her alive. Come on, we must go."

"What about my father?" Obi asked.

"I am sure he is okay, and I know exactly where he will go when he can't find us. Right now, we must go to my home and pick up the other Okutas and then head straight to Katunga."

"What's in Katunga?"

"Shango," she said, picking up her sword.

Chapter 2

From Dusk Till Dawn

Joromi, Obi's father, had been very reluctant to leave the children, but he knew it was the only chance they had of escaping.

He had led the men as far away as he could by leaving a clear trail that even a blind person could follow. Joromi had come to the edge of the forest and could overhear some men talking. Ezomo had posted men all along the forest edge to make sure no one could escape. It would be impossible to get past them without being seen or to circle back, as there were men to the front, the side, and behind him.

Joromi quietly retreated until he was out of sight, jumped on Yamyam's back and pulled himself up into a tree. Once he was seated on a branch he used his spear to give Yamyam a gentle prod, sending him running into the bushes.

The men he had seen at the edge of the forest heard the noise and, as Joromi expected, left their post and were coming to investigate. There were only two of them, which was good, but he only needed one.

He waited for the first man to pass and as the second man followed he swung down, holding on to the branch with his legs, and put him in a choke hold. The man tried to scream and signal his comrade but Joromi covered his mouth just in time. The man's comrade stopped a few yards ahead. He could have sworn he had heard something, but by the time he had turned around Joromi had pulled his unconscious friend up into the tree, out of sight.

"Ojo, Ojo," the man shouted

There was no answer, so he turned back and continued heading further into the forest.

Joromi opened the satchel around his waist and pulled out an Okuta. It was the one the children had taken from Ezomo. This wasn't the first time he had come across it and he was glad he hadn't destroyed it like he had the others.

Joromi placed the Okuta on the man's chest and recited the words.

> *"To change one must send form to dust.*
> *Okuta idan, Okuta idan.*
> *From dusk till dawn, one will change form.*
> *Okuta idan, Okuta idan."*

He repeated this several times moving the Okuta between the man's chest and his own. He began to feel a strange tingly sensation all over his body and watched as his skin turned thin and course. He put his hand up to his face and felt a rough beard had replaced his once smooth chin and his lips and nose had also changed.

Once the transformation was complete he took the Okuta and tied it around his neck. He also pulled off the man's armband and tied it around his own arm. If he was going to pull this off, every little detail would count.

Joromi jumped down from the tree and headed in the direction Yamyam had gone. He had barely taken a few steps when two men appeared in front of him, looking very angry.

"Ojo, useless man. Where did you go?"

The man shouting at him looked like the first man who had passed him under the tree.

"I heard a noise over there, oh," Joromi said, pretending to be scared and pointing over at some bushes. "It could be them."

"Move out of the way you coward," the man said.

Joromi stepped to the side allowing them to pass, but as they did he grabbed their heads from behind and slammed them hard together. Both men fell to the ground motionless. He dragged their bodies off the path and hid them behind some bushes. With this disguise he would be able to blend in, but unfortunately it looked like he had chosen someone not too popular. He would have to be very careful.

Joromi whistled for Yamyam and within seconds he came galloping around the corner but came to a sudden stop.

"It's okay Yamyam. It's me," Joromi said, moving forward and stroking him gently. "Let's go back and get Idia and the children."

Yamyam nodded happily.

It took Joromi nearly an hour to get back to the path where he had left them. He looked down and could see tracks on the ground leading through the trees. He followed them until he came to a clearing at the edge of the cliff. By the disturbed soil and freshly exposed rock, it looked like it had recently collapsed, but all he could see below was the flowing river. Joromi took a few steps back and examined the clearing more carefully and noticed a small hand print in the soil. It looked like there had been a struggle and someone had been pushed to the ground.

His heart sank. Had Ezomo captured them?

Joromi jumped on Yamyam and headed the way he had just come. He didn't want to lose his son again. He didn't want to lose any of them.

He rode Yamyam non-stop for at least an hour before he saw a group of Ezomo's men.

"Ojo, where have you been and where did you get that horse?" a man said trying to grab Yamyam's reins.

Yamyam reared back, kicking the man and sending him flying into the bushes.

"Ojo, we were waiting for you to cook us your famous jollof rice, but it is too late now, we had better get moving or Ezomo will have our heads."

Things were becoming clearer now. Ojo was not only disliked, he was also the cook. He would definitely be found out if they tasted his cooking. This could become very tricky.

"Where are Ezomo and the children?" Joromi asked casually, whilst feeding Yamyam some scraps.

"What children? They only found the princess and Ezomo is keeping her close."

Joromi tried hard to conceal his surprise.

"Ojo, go and ready our horses and stop asking useless questions. It's a long ride to Katunga, so make sure you give them enough water."

Joromi nodded obediently and walked over to where the horses were tied up and when the men were not looking he cut the ropes and released them. Just for good measure he also slashed their water bags.

"Ojo what are you doing?" shouted one of the men.

But it was too late. Joromi was riding as fast as he could out of the camp and in the direction of Katunga.

Chapter 3

Ezomo, the Past, Present and Future

Ezomo's convoy had left Shagamu and had been travelling non-stop for the last few hours.

Titi had been tied securely to the back of a donkey, but her head was hanging over its behind and every so often it received a hard bump. She had been drifting in and out of consciousness when a loud fart from her four-legged friend quickly brought her around.

"Did that wake you, princess?" asked one

of the men jokingly, whilst the others laughed and covered their noses.

Unfortunately, Titi's arms were tied so she had no way of defending herself from the foul smell. All she could do was close her eyes and turn her head to the front. After the smell had finally faded, Titi opened her eyes again. She was now facing forward and could see Ezomo riding up ahead. He was with two other men deep in conversation. She couldn't be completely sure, but she thought she recognised one of them. He looked like one of her father's friends, one of the seven province chiefs.

Titi's thoughts were disrupted by her donkey stopping abruptly. It had started a tug of war with the man trying to pull it and she could see why. Ezomo and the men ahead of her had just entered a river. Most donkeys don't like water and Titi guessed this one was no different.

With the help of another man pushing from behind, her captors managed to get the donkey into the river but nearly a third of the way out they realised they had another problem. The current was very strong and was pushing the water over the donkey's back. Titi had already swallowed a mouthful of water as she was tied down and her head was getting closer and closer to the surface of the river.

The two men began to panic as they could see Ezomo watching them angrily from the other side of the river. If Princess Titi died in their hands, there would be trouble.

One of the men made the wise decision to untie her. He had only just undone the rope around her waist when Titi gave him a hard kick, pushing him into the water. The current was so strong that within seconds it had carried him away. Titi jumped off the donkey and gave it a hard slap. It went wild, kicking the man behind it hard as it bolted back to shore. Titi took a deep breath and dived underwater. She knew the only way for her to escape was to hold her breath for as long as she could and let the current carry her.

Thanks to the commotion she had caused she had been able to cover some distance before anyone thought to follow her. The men on the river bank were too busy laughing at their two comrades, but an angry look from Ezomo quickly put a stop to that as he ordered them to get off their horses and join the search.

Titi swam as hard as she could underwater in the direction of the river bank. When she finally emerged, she was careful to keep her head down amongst the weeds.

"There she is," shouted one of Ezomo's men, spotting her immediately.

Titi got up and ran as fast as she could. She had a small head start and was going to make the most of it. The grass in the area ahead of her was very long and would make a good hiding place.

Once she had reached it she stopped, bending down to see where the men were. She was just about to get up and move again when someone grabbed her from behind. She tried to scream but quickly found a hand covering her mouth. Titi bit down hard as she felt herself being spun around.

One of Ezomo's men was kneeling down in front of her holding his finger to his lips.

"Shhh. Princess Titi it is me, Joromi," he said, wrenching his hand away from her teeth.

Titi looked confused at first but then remembered that they had given him the Okuta that could change one's appearance.

"What happened to Obi and Idia?" Joromi asked.

"Idia fell off the cliff and Obi jumped in after her. I'm not sure if either of them survived the fall," she said as her eyes began to well up with tears.

"It's okay. Right now, let's get you safe."

Joromi got up to move but as he did a spear went flying passed, missing Titi by inches.

"Ah. Ojo, what are you doing here?" shouted the man who had thrown the spear.

"Are you crazy? You nearly killed the Princess," Joromi said angrily, picking up the man's spear and stepping forward.

"Who elevated you from cook to warrior? Hand the girl over before I slap you!"

The man lunged forward but with one quick swoop Joromi cleared his legs from underneath him. By the time he hit the ground,

Joromi was standing over him, with his spear inches from his face.

"What is going on here?"

Both men looked up. It was Ezomo. He had come back from the other side of the river, not trusting his men to handle the situation on their own.

"I caught the girl, but he tried to kill her," Joromi said bowing his head and avoiding Ezomo's gaze.

"*Oga, now lie be that.* I was going to..."

"Silence! And who are you?" Ezomo asked, pointing at Joromi.

"I am Ojo," Joromi replied.

"He is the cook," the man lying on the ground added.

Ezomo laughed.

"Well, he has done a better job than you."

"Chinua and Chidera," Ezomo said,

calling his scouts, "ride ahead and request for an audience with Shango. Tell him I would like to see him about a matter of great importance and take this man Ojo with you."

"Congratulations, Ojo you are now a scout and you," he said, turning to the man still lying on the ground, "are the new cook."

The man wanted to beg, but he knew better. His punishment could have been much worse.

Joromi turned to Titi.

"Don't worry. I'll come back for you," he whispered as he handed her over to one of Ezomo's men and departed.

A few hours later, Ezomo had stopped and ordered his men to set up camp to get out of the midday sun. The new cook had been put to work and had brought some food over. Titi didn't trust him and even though she was starving she didn't touch it, just in case he had poisoned it.

"Titi you must eat," said a voice from behind her.

Titi turned to see the old chief standing behind her. He came around with his plate of food and as if he had read her mind he took her plate and gave her his.

They sat there eating quietly, neither saying a word.

"Chief Osagie, I thought you were my father's friend? Why are you working for that evil man, Ezomo?" Titi asked, finally breaking the silence.

"I have known Ezomo since he was a child. He is not evil, and I don't work for him."

"But he killed his father," Titi said. "Only an evil person would do that."

"Do not believe everything you hear or

see, my child. Our eyes and ears lie to us every day, not to talk of the eyes and ears of others," he said, looking at her sternly.

"Ezomo loved his father very much, they disagreed on many things but that does not mean he killed him. In fact, on the night Ezomo's father died he was with me. He came to me with proof of a plot his father was planning against the kingdom. At first, his father denied it but when we confronted him with the evidence he tried to get us to join him.

"Of course, we refused and immediately set off to warn your father, but we were attacked on the way and the proof of his father's deceit was stolen.

"Ezomo was angry and wanted to confront his father, but without proof there was nothing we could do, so I told him to come and spend the night at my home.

"The next morning guards turned up at my house and arrested Ezomo for the murder of his father.

"The council was called, and I tried to defend Ezomo but I was warned by the other chiefs that if I continued to do so I would be putting my family in danger.

"Ezomo was banished, but before leaving he told me that he believed the people his father was working with were responsible for his death and he would not stop until he found them.

"That is why you hear stories of him attacking people and burning villages. He wanted to avenge his father and find the evidence to prove his innocence.

"After that, no one heard from him for a very long time. Then one day he came to see me. He had finally found the evidence to clear his name.

"The plan was for us to go to Benin and reveal everything to your father but that all changed when we had a visit from a strange old man, who seemed to appear from nowhere. He had a strange stone, he called it an Okuta, and when we touched it we saw what the future might hold."

Titi guessed who the old man was but didn't say anything. She watched the expression on the chief's face turn from sadness to fear.

"The evil that is coming is more dangerous than anyone can imagine. It will take the life from under the very earth on which we stand. It will bring us to our knees and put us in chains, and when it is done with us, it will poison our minds against each other."

"It sounds like we don't have a chance. So why do you help Ezomo?"

The chief looked up.

"There is always hope my child. I do not agree with the way Ezomo goes about doing things, but we must unite if we are to stand a chance.

"Unfortunately, your father never believed in these prophecies and has wasted valuable time, ignoring them instead of preparing.

"Ezomo is preparing but not for what many people think. He does not want to take Benin for himself, he is trying to save it, and to do that we must all find a way to work together."

Titi thought carefully before saying anything. It was strange, but the pieces of this puzzle were all slowly coming together. Perhaps this is what the strange old man wanted. They all had to start working together and trust each other.

Titi leaned over to the chief.

"Have you heard of the great walls of Benin?" she asked.

Chapter 4

The Seven Okutas

Idia, Obi, and Mumu began making their way along the river until they found a path out of the forest.

They had spent at least half an hour wading around in the river looking for Idia's bag. They had hoped that it and her Map of Stars had been swept down by the current, but they had found nothing and decided to leave. Luckily, this was an area Idia travelled through often, so it wasn't too hard for her to find her bearings.

They had been trekking for an hour and Obi and Mumu were getting tired.

"Where is your home?" Obi asked. "Is it still far?"

"No, it's just over there," Idia said, pointing.

"Where?"

He could only see trees and bushes.

"Over there," she said pointing again.

All of a sudden, they broke out into a clearing and right in the middle was a peculiar looking house, with a huge tree growing out of its roof.

Idia walked over to the house and opened the door, entering into a large room with a winding staircase cut out of the trunk of the huge tree, leading up into the ceiling. She hadn't been back in such a long time and there was dust everywhere.

"This is my home, where *Baba* and I used to live," Idia said, waving Obi and Mumu in.

"This place is a mess, oh," Mumu whispered to Obi then walked off to try and find a dust free spot to sit down.

"Ah, ha," he said, finding a broom leaning against the wall.

He picked it up, gave it a good shake before laying it on the ground and taking a seat.

Idia went to the other side of the room and bent down in front of a potted plant. She gently lifted it up and pulled out a piece of cloth. She was half hoping it wouldn't be there as that would have meant Joromi had come back for it and was alive.

She put the cloth on the ground and unwrapped it. Obi was on the other side of the room looking up at the staircase when he felt his skin suddenly start to tingle. He walked over to where Idia was kneeling. She had seven Okutas laying out in front of her, much bigger than the ones he had seen, and he could feel they were much more powerful.

"What are those?" Obi asked, pointing at the symbols carved on the ends.

"Each of these Okutas holds a special kind of power and these marks show what it is and where we will need to place it to raise the great walls of Benin."

Obi was intrigued.

"So, do you know why I have Okuta in my blood and why they make me tingle?" he asked.

"Okutas are attracted to one another and share their power. Only a few people truly understand how they work. *Baba* spent his whole life studying them."

Obi listened quietly. He could see whenever she spoke of her father a look of fondness spread across her face.

"*Baba* said you would be very special," she said, smiling up at him. "He said you and the Okutas were connected."

"How did he know?"

"Because he put the Okuta in your blood."

"Eh, why? How? I don't remember meeting him."

"Oh, but you did. When you were a little child floating in your mother's womb," Idia said, laughing.

"When *Baba* visited your city many years ago, he met your mother and father. They had been trying to have children for a very long time, but your mother's womb was ill.

"You were only a few months old when

she started to have severe pains and they both thought they would lose you, that was when *Baba* gave them the Okuta dust.

"He told them the illness in her womb was spreading through her body and that the Okuta might be able to save you.

"Every night your mother drank it and she felt you growing stronger and stronger inside her, but she also felt something else, a weird tingling feeling.

"*Baba* said when Okutas are placed near each other they share their energy and that is most likely the tingling sensation you feel. For some strange reason, you can absorb the powers of any Okuta permanently if you use it once. I'm guessing that was how you were able to save me even without having the healing Okuta.

"But, Okutas also take something from you, so you must learn how to control it or you will continue to blackout or worse."

Obi could hear her words drowning out as he dreamed of the different powers he could have and what he could do with them.

He stretched his hand out to touch one of the Okutas lying on the floor between them but received a hard knock on the back of his hand for his effort.

"Aww! How am I going to learn to control it if you don't let me try?" he asked, rubbing his hand gently.

Idia hesitated.

"Okay, I'll teach you, but you must pay attention. These are very powerful and even *Baba* wasn't sure how you might react to all of them."

Idia lined up the Okutas alongside each other with their symbols facing upwards.

The first Okuta had swirly lines on it

representing water. As they watched it they could see the lines moving up and down like waves on the sea.

The second Okuta had an eye on it. Obi jumped back when it winked at him.

"That Okuta was one of *Baba*'s favourites. It is the all-seeing eye, future and past," Idia said touching it affectionately.

"She has many secrets but only tells those who are able to hear. I'm not sure this will work for you."

Idia moved her finger over to the third Okuta. It had hands, like a clock, slowly moving around in circles.

"This is the one that *Baba* used to make Queen Idia's mask, as you already know this slows down time."

The fourth Okuta had a sign that looked like fire, or an explosion carved on it and it glowed slightly more than the others. Obi stretched his hand out to touch it but Idia gave his hand another hard knock.

"Ouch! I thought you said I could try."

"I did, but not that one. Let's go with something a little less dangerous." Idia said picking up the fifth Okuta and smiling. "This will do."

The Okuta Idia had picked up had a small sprouting seed carved into it.

"Oh no! Not the baby flower one. That looks boring," Obi said.

He leaned over trying to get a look at the remaining two but Idia quickly wrapped them back up in the cloth.

"Do you want to learn or don't you?"

Obi thought for a second. There was no way Idia would teach him if he didn't play along.

"Okay, so what does it do?" he asked,

pretending to sound interested.

"It grows things."

Obi's eye lit up. Perhaps this one wasn't that boring after all.

"But it can only grow living things. Come, let's go outside. I'll show you."

Idia got up and walked outside with Obi and Mumu following closely behind her.

Once they were outside Idia looked around for some seeds that they could practice with. After finding some, Idia laid them out on the porch and used the Okuta to touch them. One by one the seeds magically popped open and started to grow, their roots stretching out, trying to find soil.

"Wow!" Obi said, honestly impressed.

"Can it do that to mangoes?" Mumu asked, licking his lips, dreaming of a garden full of gigantic fruits.

"Now, it's your turn," Idia said pushing a seed over to Obi and handing him the Okuta.

Obi stretched the Okuta out to touch the seed but Idia stopped him.

"No, absorb the power from the Okuta first and then try touching the seed with your hands."

Obi took a deep breath, closed his eyes and concentrated. After a few seconds, he opened his eyes, put the Okuta down and gently touched the seed. Nothing happened.

He picked it up and gave it a little squeeze. Still nothing.

"You have to concentrate and tell it what to do," Idia said, encouragingly.

Obi closed his eyes again and concentrated.

When he finally opened his eyes to look at the seed in his hand he was filled with disappointment. It hadn't grown a bit.

"This is useless," he said, throwing the seed down and stomping back into the house.

"Obi you need to learn to have patience or you will never master anything," Idia said following him inside.

"I'm sure you're just tired. Anyway, we had better start moving, we have a long trip ahead."

"What's up there?" Obi asked, walking over to the staircase.

"That's *Baba*'s workshop, where he carried out his experiments. Come, I'll show you quickly, but we must hurry."

She led Obi upstairs into a large room with a very low ceiling and branches stretching from one end of the room to another that also shot straight through the roof. The place was a mess and there were books everywhere, on the floor, the table and even spilling out of a hammock in the corner of the room.

Idia grabbed a bag and started packing things into it. Obi walked over to the only table in the room and picked up a small leather book. It had the picture of the sun drawn on one side and the moon on the other.

"Oh, there it is," Idia said, pulling it out of his hand, and throwing it into the bag before he had a chance to look inside.

"That is *Baba*'s secret notebook. We'll need that when you are ready to learn," she said, pushing him towards the staircase and downstairs.

Mumu had done some packing of his own but Idia didn't mind as she wasn't sure when she would be back here again. She ushered Obi and Mumu out of the house and closed the door.

As they left the clearing and headed back into the bushes, Idia could have sworn she had heard a noise but dismissed it as the wind.

Back at her home, underneath the porch, there was a loud cracking sound as one of the boards buckled and flew up into the air. A few seconds later a small seed popped its head out and slowly began to grow and grow and grow.

Chapter 5

The Orisha of Thunder and Lightning

Idia, Obi, and Mumu trekked for a short while before coming to a village. Idia was well known and it was not long before she had secured them a horse and some food for their journey.

"Have you been to the Oyo Empire before?" Obi asked.

"Yes, but a very long time ago. The road to Oyo is very dangerous you must do exactly what I say, both of you," she said, giving Mumu a stern look.

"Hopefully, we'll get there before Ezomo, and find your father."

"But how are we going to fight a god, a mighty *Orisha* like Shango?" Obi asked.

"Shango is no god. He is just a man like any other, that loves war and power, and by the way, it is the axe that gives him his power, too much power for one man. *Baba* said it was never meant to be."

"Did your *baba* know him?"

Idia laughed.

"Of course. Shango's real name is Jakuta and he is *Baba's* nephew."

"Eh?" Obi said confused.

"I told you he was no god, just a big bully. *Baba* was fonder of his older brother."

"Shango has a brother?"

"Yes, his name is Ajaka. He is very nice,

you'll like him. He is the one we are going to see. He will help us."

"Does Ajaka have powers to help us fight Shango, I mean Jakuta?"

"Obi, it is not always power one needs to defeat one's enemies."

"I know, but does he have any?" Obi asked again, impatiently.

"He had. Jakuta and Ajaka's mother was a high priestess and before she died she gave them two special Okutas. One Okuta could shine a light, bright enough to illuminate the sky and the other made a loud sound you could hear for miles.

"Ajaka, being the quieter one of the two was given the Okuta of light and Jakuta the one of sound.

"Ajaka was well liked in their town as he used his Okuta to help people find their way in the dark. This made Jakuta very jealous as he never really found a purpose for his Okuta. *Baba* told him he needed to practice more, that the power of sound was much more powerful than he could imagine but would take time to master.

"One day, while Ajaka was practicing, Jakuta came to him and asked for help but he refused. Jakuta was very angry and threw his Okuta at Ajaka and both Okutas clashed. Ajaka said there was a loud bang and bolts of lightning came down from the sky, knocking them both off their feet.

"The lightning continued, striking trees and houses and setting them alight. Sadly, many people died that day, but Jakuta and Ajaka never told anybody it was them, for fear of being killed or banished.

"After a few weeks everything went back to normal but one day Ajaka woke up and

Jakuta was gone and he had taken Ajaka's stone.

"Ajaka never heard from his brother again, but he did hear stories of an *Orisha* called Shango who could command thunder and lightning with his double-headed stone axe.

"It wasn't until one day when their kingdom was under attack and Ajaka was kidnapped that Jakuta came back and they came face to face with each other again.

"After Jakuta had rescued him and defeated his enemies he warned Ajaka to keep his identity a secret and also demanded Ajaka's throne. Ajaka wasn't happy about this but his brother was now the mighty Shango and he knew he didn't stand a chance in a fight.

"Many people have challenged Shango and lost. Some have tried to steal the axe but anyone that touches it ends up blind, deaf or even worse, dead. *Baba* once told me that there might be a chance that since half of the axe belongs to Ajaka, whatever Shango did to it won't affect him. Up until now Ajaka has had no reason to defy his brother, but once we tell him about what is going to happen he will help us get it."

"Are you sure?" Obi asked, not very convinced.

Idia didn't answer but glanced down at her sword. She hoped for Ajaka's sake that he didn't need too much persuading.

Chapter 6

The Talking Tree of Knowledge

Obi, Mumu, and Idia had been riding hard for a few hours and were on a path that cut through a large field. Idia slowed the horse down to a trot. The tall blades of grass tickled Obi's feet, making him laugh.

He was about to ask Idia something when she put her finger to her lips.

"Do you hear something?" she whispered, looking over at the trees.

"No," Obi replied.

Idia cupped her hand in front of her mouth and imitated a mating call. Birds for miles would have heard this and responded but when she stopped there was only silence.

"This is not good," she said. "Nature is never this quiet."

She was right. Nothing would stop a bird responding to a mating call, except the presence of nearby danger. Then she heard it, the faint creaking sound of a bow and arrow, but to well-trained ears like hers, it was as loud as a tree branch cracking.

"Hold on," she said, slipping on her mask.

Idia leaned forward, clicked her heels and the horse shot forward. The path they were on left them too exposed. She veered off and headed towards the trees at full speed. She turned as she rode and spotted two arrows whizzing in their direction. She slowed down slightly, watched them fly past then sped up again.

"We have to get to the trees; their bow and arrows will be less effective there. Get ready to jump down and follow me," Idia shouted.

Idia stopped just as she reached the trees and managed to avoid another arrow as it whizzed past them into a tree. She jumped down and Obi and Mumu quickly followed and within seconds they were running as fast as they could through the forest.

Idia could see movement from behind them as well as to the left and the right. Whoever they were, they were trying to cut them off. For now, the only way was forward.

Mumu had run ahead and disappeared from view, but suddenly they saw him running back towards them.

"We are surrounded, oh," Mumu said as

he scrambled up the nearest tree.

"What should we do?" Obi asked.

Idia looked around. She could see faces in the bushes all around them, there was no way they could run or fight all of them.

"Listen, Obi, do exactly what I do."

Idia fell to her knees facing the nearest tree and started chanting. Obi immediately did the same and every few seconds they bowed their heads down and then continued chanting. The men surrounding them seemed to be confused by this action and proceeded very carefully. As they came closer Idia stopped chanting and slowly stood up, making sure not to startle them.

"The tree of knowledge greets you, fellow warriors," she said in a deep bellowing voice.

The men looked at each other but said nothing.

"My name is Ayakata and I am the royal messenger of the sacred talking tree of knowledge."

This time the men looked at each other and burst out laughing.

"People do many things before they are about to die but this is a new one," one of the men said.

By this time, they had all come out of hiding.

"Talking tree of knowledge speak to them. Tell them why you have sent for them," Idia said, looking up at Mumu, who had concealed himself amongst the branches.

Mumu stared back blankly.

"Talking tree of knowledge, please speak to these warriors before they kill us. Tell them why you have sent for them."

Mumu looked down at Idia and his eyes

lit up. Ah, she wanted him to talk.

"Huh, huh," Mumu said, clearing his throat.

"Warriors of Oyo, do not harm my humble servants, oh, or my roots will come up from the ground and pull you down."

"Oh, oh," one of the men said stepping back.

"Some of you have been very naughty, shooting at my servants. Don't you know I see and hear everything?" Mumu said in the deepest voice he could muster.

One of the warriors didn't seem convinced and stepped forward.

"If you really *dey* see everything, how many fingers I *dey* hold behind my back?"

Idia was only standing a few feet away and could see three of his fingers. She looked up at Mumu trying to get his attention. When he

66

finally looked down in her direction Idia blinked three times and prayed that Mumu could count as well as he could talk.

Obi stood holding his breath.

"You are holding three dirty fingers behind your sweaty back," Mumu shouted back.

The men looked at their comrade as he revealed his fingers.

"Now, if you have finished testing my great intelligence and wisdom I would like to tell you why I have sent for you. I don't like the way you treat monkeys. You need to start treating them with more respect."

The men looked at each other confused.

"That is only one of the reasons, o wise one. Should I tell them the main reason?" Idia said interrupting.

"Err yes, you can tell them," Mumu said sadly as he could feel his talking role was coming to an end.

"We have come because of Shango," Idia said dramatically, raising her hand above her head and pretending to swing an invisible axe.

Now the men looked worried.

"We know that Shango has oppressed you and driven you from your homes. The trees of the forest are fed up too, of all his lightning and thunder. Thankfully, the talking tree of knowledge has given me the secret to Shango's power, so I may defeat him and put an end to his evil reign, so you can return home to your families."

The men were looking at each other nodding their heads in agreement.

"All the tree asks of you is that when the time comes to act, do not be scared. Come straight to the city and take your rightful place."

"But how will we know?" they asked.

"The sacred talking tree of knowledge will tell you, so stay here and wait."

"Eh," Mumu said nearly falling out of the tree.

He didn't like the sound of this plan.

Obi and Idia walked past the men. Once they were out of sight they started running as fast as they could back to where they had left their horse.

"Wow, that was close," Obi said. "But why are we running? They believed us."

"How long do you think it will take for Mumu to say something silly and get himself into trouble?" she asked, climbing on the horse and pulling Obi up.

"Run oh, run. These people *dey craze,*" Mumu shouted running out of the forest and jumping up on the horse behind them.

"What happened? Obi asked.

"I'm not sure, oh. I asked them to go and get me some pawpaws, mangoes and those nice little kiwis, so we could eat while we wait and the next thing I know they were shooting at me."

Idia gave Obi the "I told you so" look then kicked the horse and headed off towards Katunga.

Chapter 7

All Roads Lead to Katunga

By late afternoon Obi, Mumu, and Idia had reached Katunga, the great trading city and capital of the Oyo Empire. After getting directions from passers-by, they finally arrived at Ajaka's house.

"Ajaka," Idia shouted, knocking on the door but there was no answer.

"Ajaka," she called out again, a little louder this time.

"He has gone to the farm," said a woman, coming out from behind the house. "Are you his

71

friends?"

"Yes, we are very old friends."

"Oh, wonderful. Go inside, the door is open. I'll put your horse around the back. I was just going to the farm myself. I will tell him you are here."

"Thank you," Idia said.

Obi and Idia entered the house. The shutters were closed but the room was well lit. It seemed strange to have candles burning, especially during the day, but on closer inspection, they could see it wasn't the case. Spread across the shelves in the room were glass jars containing a transparent gel and trapped motionless inside them were fireflies, thousands of them magically lighting up the room.

"He must really have a lot of time on his hands," Obi said, wondering how long it must have taken to collect them all.

"Idia, my dear Idia, where have you been? Has the old man kept you locked up all this time?" Ajaka said, bursting through the door.

Idia gave him a big hug.

"I see your love for light hasn't changed," she said, pointing to the jars on the shelf.

"Ah, my little experiments. Old habits die hard and have you met anyone that doesn't love the light. One day you will find this in every house in the land and I will be rich beyond my dreams," he said laughing.

"This is Obi, the son of the great warrior Joromi," Idia said, pushing Obi forward.

"It is an honour to meet you, Obi. We used to sing songs about your father when we were younger. Idia, do you remember?"

"Yes, of course. You had a terrible singing voice. Birds used to fall out of the sky whenever you sang."

"That was not so. They came down to hear me sing," he said, laughing. "So, how is *Baba*?"

"I haven't seen him in a few years. He went on one of his journeys and has not returned, but that is not important right now. We came here to ask for your help."

Ajaka motioned for them to sit down. Idia sat, but Obi continued wandering around the room.

Idia told Ajaka about Ezomo's plans to join forces with Shango and take over the Benin kingdom. She explained the devastating consequences this would have if it happened.

"I need you to get the axe from Shango. His men will not follow him without his power," she said.

"You know Shango will not give it up without a fight. The last time we met he warned me if I ever tried to take it he would tell everyone what had happened that night. Remember, it was my stone of light that caused the fire and killed those people."

"That was years ago Ajaka and you were just a child, people forgive. Now you have a chance to make amends. If you don't, many more people will die."

"I'm sorry, but I can't help you. The people here already treat me like an outcast. They have forgotten the good I once did for this city when I ruled. They are not as forgiving as you think," he said.

Ajaka was facing the wall, but he could see Idia's hand moving towards her sword in the reflection of one of his glowing lamps. Without turning around he picked up the lamp and threw it to the ground. There was a bright flash of light as hundreds of fireflies came to life filling the room in a frenzy. Idia was blinded for a few seconds which was more than enough time for Ajaka to reach the back door and disappear.

Idia ran after him but stumbled over Obi and fell. By the time she reached outside Ajaka had vanished.

"Where do you think he has gone?" Obi asked Idia after they had searched the area with no luck.

"The only place I can think of is the temple. When we were young he used to go there and hide. We don't have much time. If he gets there before us we might never find him."

On horseback, it only took a few minutes to get to the temple and as they approached, Idia caught a glimpse of Ajaka entering the temple gates.

"Wait here," Idia said, jumping off the horse and running in after him.

The temple was dark except for a few burning torches hanging from the walls. Idia could hear footsteps to her left. She grabbed one of the torches off the wall and gave chase.

"I think we should go and help her," Obi said, climbing off the horse.

"Obi, you never listen, oh. Idia said stay here. She does not need your help. Trust me! It is Ajaka that needs help. If Idia finds him he is finished."

"That's exactly what I'm afraid of," Obi said, running off into the temple.

With so many passages Obi thought it would be impossible to find them but by following the sound of fighting he was able to locate them in minutes.

He could hear scuffling coming from around the corner and as he turned he saw Idia and Ajaka on the floor struggling. Idia was sitting on Ajaka's chest and pressing a knife towards his neck.

"Stop," Obi shouted, running forward but Idia pushed him back.

Her knife was getting closer and closer to Ajaka's neck. Obi had to do something. He grabbed the wall, closed his eyes and concentrated. This temple was very much like the hidden temple of Ogiso. There were patches of algae on the walls and weeds and small vines growing out of its cracks. Suddenly, the vines started to grow. They crept along the ground and walls heading straight for Idia and Ajaka and before either of them knew it they were being pinned against the wall with their arms and legs tied and their weapons lying harmlessly on the floor.

"Obi, put me down," Idia shouted, trying to get loose, but the vines just became tighter.

"No, you were going to kill him," Obi replied angrily.

"Of course, I wasn't. He is like a brother to me," she said, faking a smile. "I was just going to cut..."

But before she could finish Obi had collapsed to the ground.

"What is happening here, oh? What kind of witchcraft is this?" Mumu said, strolling around the corner, seeing Ajaka and Idia pinned up against the wall.

"Quick Mumu, give me my knife," Idia said, pointing towards her feet.

Mumu hesitated but decided it was better to do what she said. Within seconds she had cut herself down.

"He is not breathing," she said, leaning over Obi.

"Quickly, get me down. I can help him,"

Ajaka shouted.

Idia didn't trust him, but she didn't have much of a choice.

Once Ajaka was free he knelt over Obi and began pressing on his chest and breathing into his mouth. After a few seconds, Obi began to stir.

"His breathing is very shallow. Help me get him up. We need to get him back to my place, I have something there that will help," Ajaka said.

Idia and Ajaka carried him out and put him on the horse.

"I'll take him back," Ajaka said, climbing up behind Obi. "I need you to go and get some Moringa leaves. Be quick, he doesn't have much time."

Idia watched him as he rode off, still not sure whether she could really trust him but now she wasn't in a position not to.

*　　　　　*　　　　　*

It had been several hours since Joromi and the other men had left the camp and had been riding hard non-stop. Joromi hoped Titi would be safe. He didn't want to leave her with Ezomo's men for too long, as they were very unpredictable.

As he rode he tried to block out thoughts of what might have happened to Idia and Obi. He had to stay focused.

When they finally reached the palace, the two men riding with Joromi went to one side and started whispering to one another, then one of them got on his horse and headed off into town.

"You stay out here and water and feed the horses," said the other man as he walked towards the palace gates.

Joromi nodded obediently and watched him disappear into the palace grounds.

*   *   *

Back at his house, Ajaka had laid Obi on the floor. Obi's breathing was still very shallow, and his body was heating up so Ajaka opened the door and windows to let more air in.

Ajaka had to go to the kitchen to get a knife to cut the herbs. When he came back he knelt down in front of Obi to check on his breathing again. He was just about to get up when he heard a sound behind him, but before he could turn someone had grabbed his neck and was strangling him.

Ajaka tried to use his knife but dropped it. His vision was becoming blurry and he was running out of air. Just as he was about to black out he heard Idia whispering something, then there was a cracking noise and the grip around his neck loosened. He thought his neck had been snapped but slowly as the blood started rushing back to his head and he regained his senses he could see Idia standing over him holding his knife.

"So, are you going to kill me?" he asked, rubbing his neck.

"Of course not, but he was going to," she said pointing to the man lying next to him on the ground.

Idia had seen the intruder enter the house from a distance but by the time she had got there he was already on top of Ajaka. She had picked up the nearest object, a wooden stool, and smashed it over his head.

"Come on help me tie him up," she said, handing him his knife.

"Who is he?" Ajaka asked.

"He looks like one of Ezomo's men, but I

don't know how he found us. Let's gag him, we don't want him calling for help. We'll question him when he wakes up."

After tying the man up, they began attending to Obi. Ajaka mixed the leaves Idia had collected with his ingredients and poured the concoction down Obi's throat. Within seconds Obi was awake and running around the room, coughing, hitting his chest and making strange noises.

Idia grabbed the drink from Ajaka and tasted it.

"Eww," she said, spitting it out. "Are you trying to kill him?"

"That's the normal reaction. The taste is so disgusting it can wake the dead. It also gives a burst of energy that goes straight to the heart."

"Hey, little man, do you feel like your veins are on fire and your heart is about to explode?" Ajaka asked Obi.

Obi nodded his head vigorously.

"Then it is working. You'll be as good as new in a few minutes."

Idia looked carefully at Obi. At least he was up and running which was definitely an improvement, she thought.

"Thank you," she said, turning to Ajaka.

"You are welcome," he replied.

"Look, even if I decide to help you, how are we going to get into the palace and close enough to get the axe? The last time I saw Jakuta he said the guards should only let me back into the palace if I am in a coffin."

Idia laughed.

"Your brother was always the funny one."

"He wasn't joking," Ajaka said with a serious look on his face.

While they were talking Obi had noticed

the prisoner in the corner and wandered over and pushed the man's head. He didn't move.

"Who is this?" he asked, pushing him again.

"He is one of Ezomo's men? We'll question him later, let's get something to eat. I'm starving," Idia said.

Ajaka and Idia stood up and moved their conversation to the kitchen. Obi started to follow but then turned back and gave the man a hard kick in his side.

"That's for Titi," he said, then headed to the kitchen with Idia and Ajaka.

Mumu had been sitting quietly by the door watching the prisoner very closely. When the others had left the room, he crept over and slid his hand down the man's shirt.

"Argh. Argh."

The man growled through his gag, but

Mumu ignored him and stuck his hand further down the man's shirt and ripped off whatever was tied around the man's neck. The prisoner growled at him again, but Mumu gave him a slap, then turned and skipped happily back towards the other side of the room. He was so excited about his new acquisition that he began unwrapping the cloth immediately, but then he stopped dead in the middle of the room. Right there, in his palm was an Okuta. Mumu remembered the last time he pulled an Okuta off someone's neck and a shiver ran down his spine.

Mumu spun around expecting to see Ezomo staring at him with a spear in his hand but instead sitting there tied up with a cloth in his mouth and looking very, very angry was Joromi.

"Eh, Papa Obi, is that you?" Mumu asked.

By now Idia, Obi, and Ajaka had come out of the kitchen and were staring at Joromi tied up, right where their prisoner used to be. It was only when they saw the Okuta in Mumu's hand that it started to make sense.

Obi was the first to run over and give his father a big hug.

"You're alive," he said pulling the cloth out of his father's mouth and untying him.

"Barely," Joromi said rubbing his head and ribs as Obi tried hard to avoid eye contact.

"Thankfully, you are too. But how?"

"It's a long story, we'll tell you over some food," Obi said, quickly getting up and going into the kitchen.

Idia came over and helped him up.

"Glad to see you alive, old friend," she said smiling, "and this is my dear friend Ajaka, the one you tried to strangle."

"Nice to meet you Ajaka, sorry about that," Joromi said, bowing slightly.

"No problem. It's not every day your closest friend and a total stranger try to kill you. Welcome to my home."

Joromi looked a bit confused.

"You tried to kill him too?" Joromi asked looking over at Idia.

"It wasn't like that. I'll explain later, let's eat," she said running off to join Obi in the kitchen.

Chapter 8

The Battle of Lightning and Thunder

Ajaka, Idia, Joromi and Obi all sat around the kitchen table, eating and talking for hours, each telling the story of how they had ended up there.

Joromi told them how he had gone back to look for them in the forest and had believed Ezomo had captured them until he had found Titi.

He then told them of his surprise when he found Obi in Ajaka's house with a man kneeling over him holding a knife. The rest of the story they all knew.

"We now have two very serious problems," Joromi said, leaning forward.

"Since Mumu has removed my Okuta I am no longer disguised and cannot get back into Ezomo's camp and rescue Titi as I had planned."

Mumu gave a little sniffle from the other side of the room. He was standing in the corner with his hands on his head. This was the punishment Joromi had given him for now. Mumu hadn't complained as he felt really bad after realising the trouble his greedy action had caused.

"Without the disguise, it also means I cannot get into Shango's palace."

"I think I have an idea of how we can do that," Idia said after some silence. "Ajaka can get us in."

"I told you I can't unless you are planning on killing me and carrying my dead body through the palace gates."

"That's exactly what we are going to do," she replied.

Ajaka froze. He glanced towards the door wondering whether or not he would be able to make it out before they could catch him.

"Hey," Idia said, seeing the fear in his eyes.

"We won't really kill you, we'll just make it look like you're dead. Remember, we need you to get the axe and for that we need you alive," she said, smiling at him, but Ajaka did not smile back.

They all sat and listened as Idia explained her plan in detail and then discussed how they would get Titi back. By the time they had finished it was dark outside.

To make Idia's plan work they would have to cover Ajaka with blood and make it look like he had been attacked and Joromi would take him to the palace. It would be up to Idia, Obi and Mumu to get Titi out.

After saying their farewells, they all set off. This plan relied heavily on timing, so they had to get into position and be ready.

Idia, Obi, and Mumu would have to scout the road leading to the city and find where Ezomo and his men had set up camp. They would then have to wait until Ezomo had left for the palace. Joromi was sure he wouldn't take Titi to the palace with him, so she would be less protected as Ezomo would be escorted by his best warriors.

Joromi and Ajaka were hiding behind some bushes not too far from the palace gates.

They would have to wait for Ezomo to enter before they carried out their part of the plan.

"Idia speaks very highly of you. I understand your reluctance to help us, but do not worry, I promise not to hurt Shango," Joromi said.

Ajaka laughed.

"It is not him I am worried about. Shango does not take betrayal lightly. If we do not succeed neither of us will leave the palace alive.

"The axe of thunder and lightning is the most powerful thing I have ever come across in my whole life, that is, until today. Your son has a great power within him, way beyond that of any Okuta, but there is something *Baba* didn't tell you about his powers."

Before Ajaka could continue the sound of drums came bellowing out from behind the palace's gates, which could only mean one thing.

Joromi peered over the bushes and could see a large party was approaching the gate. It was Ezomo and his men.

Joromi and Ajaka waited for some time before heading towards the gate. Ajaka was lying in the back of a cart, trying not to move as Joromi pulled him along.

"Please, help oh," Joromi shouted as he approached. "Ajaka has been killed."

"So why are you bringing him here?" the guard asked blocking him.

"Because he is Shango's brother."

The guard looked at him and laughed.

"That man," he said pointing to the supposedly dead Ajaka, "was a drunk, palm wine maker, and a cheat. He sold me watered down palm wine several times and by the way, Shango has no brother, he is a god, so watch your tongue."

Ajaka had warned Joromi this might happen as nobody knew of their relationship after Shango's return.

Joromi walked around the cart and pulled back Ajaka's shirt revealing a large lightning like birthmark across his chest, undeniable proof of their connection. The guard nearly choked as he shouted for another guard to come over and see. Only one other person had a birthmark like that and it was Shango.

"I think he was killed because of this," Joromi continued. "Before he died in my arms, he said I should bring his body here and warn Shango that men are coming here to try and kill him. He mentioned a name, Ezomo."

The guards looked at each other.

"Quick open the gate," they shouted.

As soon as the gates opened one of them ran inside, heading straight to the palace. The other guard ushered Joromi through.

"Wait here," he said as he walked over to another guard to gossip.

Ajaka had been trying very hard to hold his breath, but as soon as there was no one nearby he breathed out heavily.

"This blood smells, oh. I think I'm going to be sick."

"You had better not or we'll both be dead before we even get into the palace. It won't be much longer now. Just be ready, remember we'll only have one chance," Joromi whispered.

After a few minutes, the guard came running back with two other men. He ordered them to pull the cart.

"Come with me. Shango wants to see you, immediately!" he said.

They were led into the palace and then into a large dimly lit hall. At the furthest end, they could see Shango sitting upon a majestic throne. There were a group of men standing in front of him with their backs towards him. He was sure one of them was Ezomo but Joromi had to make sure he wasn't recognised, so he bowed his head and pretended to concentrate on pushing the cart forward.

Shango stood up and the men in front of him parted as he headed towards the back of the hall to meet with the stranger who had brought his dead brother to him.

"How did this happen?" Shango asked, looking down at his brother's lifeless body.

"A man came to the farm and attacked him," Joromi said, stepping forward and obscuring Shango's view.

"I was too far away to help but was able to grab this off the man as he rode away."

Joromi handed Shango the armband he

had taken off Ojo in the forest.

"Before your brother died he said I should warn you that a man called Ezomo is going to come here and try to kill you."

Shango turned around and looked at the men who had just come into his chamber asking for his help. They all wore this same armband Joromi had handed him.

"Seize them," Shango shouted, to his guards.

Before Ezomo and his men could react, they were surrounded.

At the same time, on the outskirts of the city, Idia had found Ezomo's camp. It was much larger than Joromi had described. She definitely wouldn't have been able to fight her way in and out of there, but luckily she didn't need to.

"Obi, are you ready?" Idia asked.

Obi nodded.

Ajaka had given them two small candle-like sticks, made of a soft clayey material, with a piece of rope sticking out of one end. He called them his thunder sticks and said that if you light the rope there would be a big bang and an explosion, which would destroy anything near them. Idia could tell Ajaka had not really given up on getting his stone back. His whole life seemed to be surrounded by making artificial thunder and lightning.

Obi and Mumu ran off into the darkness. They needed to find a good place to light these thunder sticks and draw out Ezomo's men while Idia rescued Titi.

"Over here," Obi said, beckoning to Mumu.

Obi had found a large pile of wood stacked against a tree. They lit the stick and shoved it underneath.

101

Idia had told them after lighting the first one, to head towards the palace and when they were halfway there they should light the second one, then go back to Ajaka's house and wait.

Idia heard a loud bang from the other side of the camp. That was her cue. She slipped on her mask and headed towards the camp. The guards had definitely been startled by the sound but only a few of them had gone to investigate. Idia was less than a few minutes into the camp when she heard a noise from behind her.

"Psst, psst!"

Idia turned. Tied up against a tree, just feet from her was Titi, smiling.

"You're alive!" Titi said.

"Yes," Idia said, running over to her.

Idia knelt down and started cutting her ropes.

"What of Obi?"

"He is fine. Once I get you out of here we'll go and meet him," she said, cutting the last rope.

"Come on, this way."

"No, wait," Titi said, running in the opposite direction and towards where the horses and donkeys were tied up.

She went over to the donkey she had been tied to and grabbed a bag off its back and opened it.

"Yes," she said, pulling out the Map of Stars. "Now, we can go."

"Oh, oh! We have company," Idia said.

Through the eyes of the mask, Idia could see they were about to be surrounded. She jumped on one of the horses and pulled Titi up.

"Get off the horse or I will shoot you," said a man coming out of the darkness, pointing a bow and arrow at them.

"Three," Idia said.

"I said, get down."

"Two."

"What is two? I said get down or I will shoot you."

"One."

The man pulled back the bow but before he could release it there was a big explosion behind him lighting up the night sky. It was much bigger than the first one and this time you could hear screams.

The man turned for a split second, but that was all Idia needed. She kicked the horse and shot forward knocking the man to the ground and disappeared into the night.

*   *   *

Obi and Mumu had successfully set off the first thunder stick, but it hadn't all gone according to plan. After they had lit the first, smaller stick they had waited to see it go off. That was a big mistake. The sound and explosion were much bigger than they expected, and Obi and Mumu were knocked clean off their feet. By the time they had recovered they could hear Ezomo's men heading in their direction.

They got up and ran as fast as they could towards the palace but within minutes the men had nearly caught up with them.

"Light the other one now," Obi shouted to Mumu holding out the stick.

Mumu lit it and Obi threw it high into the air behind them.

First came the bang, then the ground shook, swaying them from the left to the right, but this time they managed to stay on their feet. Neither Obi nor Mumu turned around, they just kept on running as loud screams came from the men behind them.

*   *   *

In the palace, Shango's guards were just about to seize Ezomo and his men when they heard the second big explosion. The sound resonated through the palace and distracted the guards giving Ezomo and his men a chance to draw their weapons.

"Now," Joromi whispered.

Ajaka climbed out of the cart and darted into the shadows, but Shango must have heard him because he turned around, grabbed Joromi by his neck and raised him off his feet. Even without his axe he was still unbelievably strong.

"Where is he?" Shango shouted.

Joromi didn't answer.

"Today, he will really die and so will you," he said, throwing Joromi backwards into the empty cart.

Shango turned and started heading back towards his throne. He knew what Ajaka was looking for, but before he had reached half way he felt a heavy hand on his shoulder and was spun around.

"Shango, stop. We didn't come here to fight you. Ezomo and his men are your enemies. What they want will cause chaos and war."

"I love war," Shango said lunging at Joromi again but this time Joromi stepped to the side, swinging his fist at Shango's head as he passed.

Even though Joromi was only half Shango's size, his fists were like rocks and Shango felt it.

"For that, I will kill you slowly," Shango said rubbing his jaw and smiling.

"Stop!" Ajaka shouted from the other side of the room.

Shango turned to see a bolt of lightning jump out of Ajaka's hand, fly around the room and land back in his hand. Ajaka had his axe of thunder.

The room was silent, but only for a second, then there was a mighty roar as Shango charged across the room, knocking everyone in his path away like flies. Ajaka stretched out the axe and pointed it at Shango, ready to launch a bolt of lightning straight at his brother's heart, but just as he was about to unleash its power, he stopped. He couldn't kill his brother. There was a loud bang and a flash of light as Shango and Ajaka collided, sending both of them flying across the hall and crashing into the wall.

Ezomo's men decided to take this opportunity to exit the palace, but Ezomo himself was doing the opposite. He was down on his knees crawling around looking for something. It was only when Joromi got to within a few feet of him he realised what Ezomo was looking for but by then it was too late. In Ezomo's hand were two large flat Okutas, which were once part of Shango's legendary axe of thunder. The handle had shattered to pieces, but the stones were intact.

Ezomo looked at Joromi as he raised the stones above his head.

"Don't," shouted Shango and Ajaka from behind him.

Ezomo slammed the two stones together and just like Ajaka and Jakuta had seen when they were children, a bright flash of light lit up the night sky and bolts of lightning came raining down, from above. Before they knew it the palace was on fire but the worst was yet to come. It sounded like the beating of a thousand drums, all at once. It rang out for miles and with it came a blast of air destroying everything in its wake and within seconds the walls of the palace came crumbling down on top of them.

*   *   *

Obi and Mumu had been running back to Ajaka's home when they saw the lightning strike the palace and saw it collapse to the ground. Obi knew they were instructed to go back to Ajaka's house, but he couldn't.

They were halfway towards the palace when they met Idia and Titi, who had also seen the lightning.

Obi and Mumu gave Titi a big hug, glad to see her alive and well.

"Do you think anyone survived?" Obi asked.

Idia didn't reply. She didn't want to lie to him. She pulled them onto the horse, slipped on her mask and rode as fast as she could towards what was left of the burning palace.

The End .....for now!

Vocabulary

Banish - 1) to send someone away from a country or place as an official punishment, or

2) to get rid of.

Example: After stealing from the village the man was banished to a deserted island.

Beckon - to make a gesture with the hand, arm, or head to encourage or instruct someone to approach or follow.

Example: As Dami was making her way out the door she beckoned to her son because she needed his help in the kitchen.

Commotion - a disturbance that is noisy and somewhat confused.

Example: As Mary walked home from school

she became distracted by the commotion of a car accident and was late getting home.

Comrade - a colleague or a fellow member of an organization.

Example: Femi respected his team members and when they needed help, he quickly joined his comrades.

Confront - 1) to come face-to-face with someone with hostile or argumentative intent, or

2) to deal with a problem or difficulty.

Example: After Kemi's brother teased her she confronted him and told him that she didn't like what he said.

Convoy - a group of ships or vehicles travelling together, typically one accompanied by armed troops, warships, or other vehicles for protection.

Example: It was safer for them to travel in a convoy across the desert to ensure that they arrived at their destination safely.

Hurtling - to move at high speed usually in an uncontrolled manner.

Example: The children were playing at the top of the mountain when they tripped and fell and came hurtling down the mountainside.

Imitate - to copy.

Example: Carla really liked Claire's accent and soon started to imitate her.

Oppress - to treat people in such a way that they are restricted by cruel or unjust rules, impositions or restraints.

Example: The citizens of their country were oppressed by their president who wouldn't let them speak freely.

Retreat - 1) to move back or withdraw, or

2) to withdraw to a quiet place, or

3) to change one's mind or plans after difficulty.

Example: After their argument David turned away and retreated to his room to think about what he had said.

Satchel - a bag carried on the shoulder by a long strap and closed by a flap.

Example: The school bell rang, indicating that it was home time, so the children put their books, pens and pencils in their satchels and started to make their way home.

Transformation - a marked change.

Example: The children were fascinated to learn of the transformation of their pet caterpillar into a butterfly.

African Facts

1. The Oyo Empire was an ancient West African Kingdom, located in present day Nigeria. It was established around 1400 and grew to become one of the largest West African states. Its most successful period was from 1650 to 1750. Its decline started in 1754 and by 1896 it ceased to exist.

2. The capital city of the Oyo Empire was Oyo-Ile also known as Katunga or Old Oyo.

3. Orisha is a very complex African concept but has spread as far as Latin America. It combines spirituality, power, nature and human form.

4. Shango (also known as Jakuta by the Yorubas) was one of the early kings of the Oyo Empire. After he died his followers believed he was taken up into heaven and transformed into a god. He was deified by his people and became the god of thunder and lightning and is still worshipped today.

5. Oba Ajaka, the Alaafin of Oyo (Alaafin means 'owner of the palace' in Yoruba), ruled the Oyo Empire before Shango and was reinstated after Shango's death.

If you liked this book, please leave a review on Amazon and we'll keep on writing more exciting adventures, just for you.

Book 6: Adventures of Obi and Titi

The Great Walls of Benin

To find out more about upcoming events, book releases and special offers, subscribe to our newsletter at:

www.obiandtiti.com

Made in the USA
Lexington, KY
29 December 2018